WIL

FLASH POINTS

LIFTOFF!

Space Exploration

Eleanor Cardell

Liftoff!
Flash Points

Copyright © 2018
Published by Full Tilt Press
Written by Eleanor Cardell

Full Tilt Press
42982 Osgood Road
Fremont, CA 94539
readfulltilt.com

Full Tilt Press publications may be purchased for educational, business, or sales promotional use.

Editorial Credits
Design and layout by Sara Radka
Copyedited by Renae Gilles

Image Credits
Newscom: MCT, 5; Shutterstock: 6 (top), 6 (bottom), 11, 23, 39, 42 (bottom); NASA: 7, 10, 12, 15, 16 (top), 16 (bottom), 17 (top), 17 (bottom), 18, 19, 21, 22, 23, 25, 26 (top), 26 (bottom), 27 (top), 27 (bottom), 30, 32 (top), 32 (bottom), 37 (top), 37 (middle), 37 (bottom), 38, 41, 42 (top); Newscom: akg-images, 7, 8; Getty Images: iStockphoto, 9; Newscom: WENN, 12; Shutterstock: Songquan Deng, 13; Newscom: Sovfoto Universal Images Group, 20; Newscom: UPI, 28; Newscom: 29; Newscom: Courtesy Everett Collection, 31; Newscom: World History Archive, 35; Shutterstock: Christopher Halloran, 36; Newscom: Atlas Photo Archive/NASA, 40; Newscom: SIPA USA/SIPA, 43

ISBN: 978-1-62920-604-2 (library binding)
ISBN: 978-1-62920-616-5 (eBook)

Contents

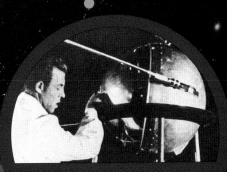

Sputnik
4

Apollo 11
14

Challenger
24

Spirit &
Opportunity
34

SPUTNIK

October 4, 1957

The fuel in the rocket starts to burn. It blasts off toward space. **Engineers** wait to find out if they've succeeded. Then, a radio signal comes through, loud and clear. Russia, known as the USSR, has successfully sent the first man-made object into orbit around Earth. It is called *Sputnik 1*.

The United States is shocked. Nobody thought the USSR would be the first to put a **satellite** into **orbit**. But people are also excited. They can use homemade radios to pick up *Sputnik*'s signal as it flies overhead. They can watch it with binoculars, a spot of light in the sky.

Sputnik can't do very much. It is silver, and about the size of a beach ball. It has three antennae sticking out from it. It weighs less than 200 pounds (91 kilograms). All it can do is send radio signals. But that is not what's important about it. *Sputnik* is something totally new.

engineer: someone who designs and builds machines

satellite: a smaller object that orbits a larger object in space

orbit: the path that something follows as it travels around something else

Sputnik orbited about 360 miles (579 kilometers) above Earth.

How and Why

Historical events rarely have only one simple cause. Many different things—such as certain events or changing ways of thinking—work together to shape the future. Take a moment to explore some of the things that led to the launch of *Sputnik*.

A New Frontier

In the 1950s, the possibility of exploring space was an exciting new concept. People thought of the future when they thought of space travel.

Cold War

The year 1947 marked the beginning of the Cold War. This was a time of fear and tension between the US and the USSR. The two countries were both trying to develop more powerful technology. They were especially interested in rockets. They needed rockets to fire missiles.

Satellites

The USSR wanted to use a satellite to send communication signals. This would allow them to talk from all over the world. But first they needed to put a satellite into space. Many scientists worked day and night. They needed to build a satellite that worked. They also needed a rocket to put it into orbit.

Race to Space

In July 1955, the US made an announcement: By the end of 1958, they would launch a satellite into space. The USSR couldn't let them win. Less than a week later, they also made an announcement. The USSR said that they would launch a satellite very soon. The race to space had begun.

What Happened Next

The USSR didn't just launch a satellite into space. It also launched the "Space Race." Before the launch of *Sputnik*, the USSR and the US both wanted to move science forward. They wanted to travel to space. At first, both countries mainly studied rocket science. Nothing can be sent into space without a rocket. After a rocket was created, then they could build things to put on the rocket.

The Cold War was a very scary time. The US was afraid of the USSR. Many people thought the USSR would use their rockets to fire a missile at the US. The US had also been building new rockets. However, they hadn't been as successful as the USSR. The US needed to build better rockets if they wanted to catch up to the USSR.

The US began to give more money to the military. They wanted the military to build rockets. They also gave money to space programs. These programs would build satellites. But these groups did not work together. The US realized that this needed to change. The next step was to create an organization that was in charge of space science.

A model of *Sputnik* hangs in the Smithsonian Institute's National Air and Space Museum, in Washington, D.C.

DID YOU KNOW?
It took *Sputnik* 98 minutes to travel around Earth.

Ripple Effects

A single event, no matter how big or small it may seem at the time, can have a big impact on the future. The launch of *Sputnik* had many far-reaching effects.

Cause for Concern

With the launch of *Sputnik*, the USSR proved that it could send objects into space. Countries around the world were worried. Governments began to spend more money. A lot of this money was spent on the military. Many countries created space programs as well. Everyone wanted to put satellites into space.

NASA

In the US, many different groups were working on space projects. The US needed to bring those groups together. The government decided to do something. In July 1958, it founded the National Aeronautics and Space Administration (NASA).

Big Changes

Sputnik's launch caused big changes in science. Many of these changes were in computer science. For example, **microelectronics** were built to be used in satellites, rockets, and spaceships. But today, they are also used in phones, computers, TVs, and more.

Studying Science

The United States wanted to catch up to the USSR. They needed to teach kids science and math. Many children wanted to be scientists. Schools began to give more attention to math and science classes.

microelectronics: very small electronic circuits and parts

DID YOU KNOW?

The US launched their first satellite on January 31, 1958. It was named *Explorer*.

In 1958, the United States began training its first astronauts. This first astronaut program was called Mercury.

SPACE JUNK

Today, many different countries have satellites. There are thousands of satellites circling Earth. Sometimes, a satellite will stop working. When that happens, there is no way to get it back. These satellites become "space junk." There are more than half a million pieces of space junk around Earth. These objects are moving very fast. They might hit a space shuttle. If they do, they could damage it. This would also hurt people on board. Today, many countries are trying to figure out how to clean up the space junk.

The Age of Space

Sputnik's launch was a big deal. People gathered near their radios. They listened to the satellite beep as it circled Earth. Some people stood outside. They could watch it fly by. It was just a speck of light in the sky. Everybody knew that the world had changed.

Sputnik's launch began the Space Age. Many governments worked together to build spacecraft. That is still happening today.

Many countries decided to give more money to space science. Schools improved their science and math programs. They taught more science and math classes. TV sets, satellite television, cell phones, and computers were all created because of the Space Race. The United States founded NASA. NASA is in charge of the US space program. Today, the US has the most successful space program in the world.

The space program brought the American people together. The country started to think that space travel could be possible. The US gave more money to military and space research. They began to build better rockets and satellites. Their satellites could do more than *Sputnik*. The US took the lead in the Space Race, but *Sputnik* will always be remembered as one of the first major advances in space technology.

DID YOU KNOW?
In January 1958, *Sputnik* started to fall back toward Earth. As it fell, it burned up.

APOLLO 11

July 20, 1969

For the past three days, three astronauts have been traveling through space. Finally, they have safely arrived at the Moon. Two of them prepare to climb out of the *Apollo 11* **lunar module**. These astronauts will be the first people to walk on the Moon.

The Moon landing is being aired on live TV. In New York, it is almost 11 p.m. Families huddle around borrowed televisions. Kids stay up past their bedtimes. Space travel has been in the news for years. This is what everyone has been waiting for. This is an event that no one wants to miss.

A camera on the outside of the spacecraft sends video back to Earth. The world watches as the hatch opens. The first astronaut, Neil Armstrong, climbs out. He jumps down from the bottom of the ladder. He pauses, then says, "One small step for a man, one giant leap for mankind." For the first time ever, there is a man on the Moon.

lunar module: a spacecraft used to transport astronauts to the surface of the Moon

manned: a flight that has a human crew on board

There are six American flags on the Moon—one for each **manned** visit to the Moon's surface.

DID YOU KNOW?

The astronauts of *Apollo 11* spent 21 hours on the Moon's surface. Only 2.5 of those hours were spent outside the lunar module.

How and Why

Historical events rarely have only one simple cause. Many different things—such as certain events or changing ways of thinking—work together to shape the future. Take a moment to explore some of the things that led to the successful landing of *Apollo 11*, and the first man to set foot on the moon.

German Rockets

After World War II ended in 1945, the US brought many German scientists over from Europe. German rockets were more powerful than US rockets. The US wanted the German scientists to help make rockets. They also helped to build new weapons.

Presidential Influence

In May 1961, President John F. Kennedy gave an important speech. He wanted the US to put a man on the Moon by 1970. He said space "may hold the key to our future." He wanted to make space exploration more important.

Catching Up

In 1957, the USSR was the first country to send a satellite into space. They were also the first to send a man into space, in 1961. His name was Yuri Gagarin. The US was falling behind in the Space Race. They wanted to be the first to put a man on the Moon.

First Orbit

The US sent a spaceship into orbit around the Moon in 1968. It was the first mission to orbit an object other than Earth. It had three astronauts. They took one of the most famous pictures of Earth. It is called "Earthrise."

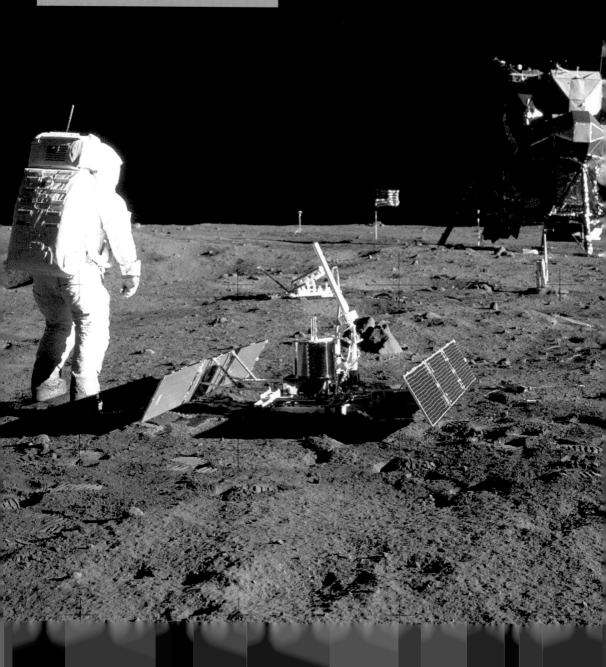

The astronauts who landed on the moon brought experiments with them. One of these is still working today.

What Happened Next

The United States was very afraid of the USSR. People were very divided. But the Moon landing affected everyone. The American people could be proud that the US put a man on the moon. They could watch it on their TV screens. It was a real victory.

The Moon landing changed the world. Science fiction was very popular. The Moon landing made books and TV shows about space travel more popular. Many children watched the Moon landing late at night. Later they studied science. The successful Moon landing made people believe that the US space program was the best in the world.

The Moon landing was very important for science. The astronauts brought back lots of rock and soil from the Moon. NASA labs studied these samples and learned a lot about the Moon. They even discovered some clues about how the Moon was formed. The Moon landing ended the Space Race. The United States had won. It was not the end of space travel, though.

DID YOU KNOW?

In 1969, President Richard Nixon awarded the Presidential Medal of Freedom to all three *Apollo 11* astronauts.

Ripple Effects

A single event, no matter how big or small it may seem at the time, can have a big impact on the future. The successful landing of *Apollo 11* and Neil Armstrong's first steps on the moon had many far-reaching effects.

Space Race

Russia, then known as the USSR, had been winning the Space Race. They'd put the first satellite into orbit. They'd sent the dog Laika into space. And they'd sent the first human into space. The US was falling behind. But then, American Neil Armstrong put the first footprint on the Moon. Finally, the US took the lead in the Space Race.

Funding

The space program had been having problems. However, after the success of *Apollo 11*, it was given more money so it could continue its work. There were five more manned missions to the Moon. They were all part of the Apollo program. In total, 12 people have walked on the surface of the moon.

Technology

Rockets became more complicated. NASA needed more complicated computers to fly the rockets. NASA gave money to research for microchips. This technology spread. Companies got better at making microchips. Because of this, building computers became less expensive. Soon, computers became more affordable for everyone.

Rocket Fuel

In the 1950s, '60s, and '70s, many different groups were studying rocket fuel. They wanted to figure out which fuel was the best. NASA created more powerful rockets. These rockets could carry more weight on less fuel.

DID YOU KNOW?

The US spent about $20 billion on the Apollo missions. Today, that much money would be worth about $100 billion.

The End of the Race

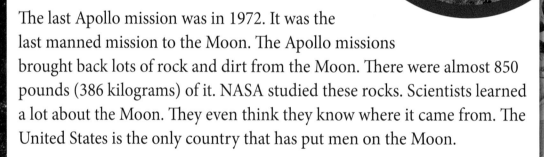

The Moon landing changed the world. *Apollo 11* gave the United States something to be proud of. Exciting technology was created thanks to the Moon landing. The *Apollo 11* rockets were the most powerful rockets in the world. Scientists used them to build even more powerful rockets. These rockets are used today. The computers used to fly the rockets were also new technology.

The last Apollo mission was in 1972. It was the last manned mission to the Moon. The Apollo missions brought back lots of rock and dirt from the Moon. There were almost 850 pounds (386 kilograms) of it. NASA studied these rocks. Scientists learned a lot about the Moon. They even think they know where it came from. The United States is the only country that has put men on the Moon.

Today, most of the world is interested in Mars. Many missions are sent to study Mars. However, the Moon hasn't been forgotten. NASA is making plans to send a manned mission to orbit the Moon. This mission would be used to study space travel. Someday they hope to send a human to Mars.

DID YOU KNOW?
The Moon is drifting away from the Earth. Every year, it gets almost 1.5 inches (3.8 centimeters) farther away.

All of the Apollo missions were monitored from the NASA Mission Control Center in Houston, Texas.

H-14

THE MOON'S ORIGIN

Scientists have many different ideas about where the Moon came from. Most scientists believe that another planet hit the Earth. This would have happened about 4.5 billion years ago. Their idea is that the other planet was smaller than Earth—about the size of Mars. When the two planets smashed into each other, lots of dust and rocks would have been thrown into space, spinning very fast. All the dust and rocks would have stuck together. When they stuck together, they formed the Moon.

CHALLENGER

January 28, 1986

The Florida morning is cold. The space shuttle *Challenger* is at the Kennedy Space Center. It is ready to launch. **Technicians** check the rockets. Seven astronauts climb into the shuttle. *Challenger* has taken off nine times before. Everybody expects this launch to work.

The space shuttle takes off. Immediately, one of the rockets starts to smoke. People from all over the US watch. Something is wrong. The space shuttle breaks apart 1 minute and 13 seconds after it launched. The pieces fall from the sky. They land in the Atlantic Ocean.

All seven astronauts died. The US Navy found the shuttle more than two months later. Some of the astronauts were buried in Arlington National Cemetery in Virginia. Others were buried in their hometowns.

technician: someone who looks after technical equipment

Smoke from the *Challenger* could be seen all the way across Florida.

DID YOU KNOW?

The space shuttle *Challenger* first took off in 1983. It was the second shuttle in NASA's Space Shuttle Program.

How and Why

Historical events rarely have only one simple cause. Many different things—such as certain events or changing ways of thinking—work together to shape the future. Take a moment to explore some of the things that led to the disasterous *Challenger* mission.

Space Shuttles

The Apollo missions to the Moon had gone very well. The US government wanted more space missions. It decided to build five space shuttles. Every shuttle could be reused. The first shuttle took off in 1981.

Too Cold

This was the Space Shuttle *Challenger*'s 10th launch. It had been delayed five times. Scientists said that the weather was bad. They said the same thing the morning of the accident. The scientists knew that it was too cold. Some parts of the rockets would not work the right way. But the shuttle was launched anyway.

Broken O-Ring

There are rockets on the shuttle. The rockets are sealed with O-rings, small circles of rubber that create a seal between two pieces of metal. Because it was cold, the O-rings were not very flexible. One of them broke during liftoff. Burning fuel escaped from the rocket. This put stress on the shuttle. It broke into pieces.

Impatience

There was an investigation after the accident. It found that NASA managers had made bad decisions. They didn't listen when scientists told them that the launch was dangerous. They didn't want to delay the launch again.

What Happened Next

The United States was very upset. Television showed videos of the disaster. It was played over and over again on the news. One of the *Challenger* astronauts who got the most media attention was Christa McAuliffe. She'd been on talk shows before the launch. The people loved her.

That night, President Reagan planned to give the **State of the Union** speech. Instead, he talked about the *Challenger* crew. He wanted to comfort the nation. Even though there had been a disaster, people couldn't lose hope. He promised that the space program would go on.

President Reagan put together a **committee**. It was led by William Rogers. It was known as the Rogers Commission. Its job was to figure out why the shuttle came apart. The Navy immediately began to search for the shuttle's wreckage. They pulled many pieces out of the ocean. Many scientists studied the pieces of the shuttle. They wanted to understand what caused the disaster.

State of the Union: a speech given by the US president to the US Congress, usually delivered once a year

committee: a group of people chosen for a specific reason, or to accomplish a specific task

President Reagan, along with his staff, watched a recording of the *Challenger* disaster on television. Later that night, he encouraged the nation to not give up in the face of this disaster.

DID YOU KNOW?

Neil Armstrong, the first man to walk on the Moon, was one of the thirteen members of the Rogers Commission.

Ripple Effects

A single event, no matter how big or small it may seem at the time, can have a big impact on the future. The *Challenger* disaster had many far-reaching effects.

Dangerous

Once, America had been excited about space travel. Now, the people saw that it could be dangerous. They began to wonder if they needed a space program.

Program End

After the *Challenger* disaster, the US Space Shuttle Program stopped. It didn't start again for almost three years. No more shuttles went into space. Scientists and engineers needed to find out what had caused the disaster. They didn't want another space shuttle to break apart.

Safety Rules

The scientists discovered that an O-ring hadn't worked right. This had caused the shuttle to break apart. NASA scientists changed their rockets. They also put new safety rules in place. If there was an emergency, the astronauts would be able to escape.

Feynman's Report

Richard Feynman was a famous scientist. He was also a member of the Rogers Commission. He discovered that NASA managers had made bad decisions. The managers had known that the launch was dangerous. They had let the shuttle fly anyway. Feynman's report included those details.

DID YOU KNOW?

NASA's Space Shuttle Program ended in July 2011. *Atlantis* was the last space shuttle to land.

In 2004, all seven *Challenger* astronauts were **posthumously** awarded the Congressional Space Medal of Honor.

TEACHERS IN SPACE

There were seven astronauts on the *Challenger*. One of them was named Christa McAuliffe. She was a teacher. She was also the first member of NASA's Teachers in Space program. Christa planned to teach classes from space. These would be filmed and shown to children. She hoped children would study science. After the *Challenger* disaster, the Teachers in Space program stopped. It was started again in 2007. Barbara Morgan was the first teacher in space.

Never Forgotten

The *Challenger* disaster was the most public space-travel tragedy in history. Millions of people watched it on TV. The crew were celebrities. Their deaths were shocking. No one expected the shuttle to break apart. NASA had thought it would work. Instead, it changed people's views of the space program.

Before the *Challenger* disaster, the space program was very popular. But afterward, people began to wonder whether they needed space travel at all. President Reagan had told people not to lose hope. But people were still upset. Seven astronauts had died. Space seemed like a very dangerous place.

Nobody wanted a disaster like that to happen again. Many people came together to decide what they needed to do. They made many changes to the space program. Shuttles and rocket boosters were changed. So were NASA rules. Today, space shuttles are much safer. The space program is much stronger.

posthumous:
happening after someone's death

DID YOU KNOW?
Sally Ride was the first American woman in space. Her first space flight was on the space shuttle *Challenger* in June 1983.

Spirit & Opportunity

January 4, 2004

The control room at the Jet Propulsion Laboratory, in Pasadena, California, is quiet. Scientists are waiting. Their eyes are glued to the screen on the wall. They're watching for a signal. It was sent all the way from Mars. They worked on this for years. They spent billions of dollars on it. Nobody wants it to fail. Finally, the signal arrives. Everybody cheers. *Spirit*, their second **rover** ever, is standing on the surface of another planet.

Three weeks later, *Opportunity* lands. It is on the other side of Mars. *Opportunity* is *Spirit*'s twin. It takes about six months to travel to Mars. Landing on Mars is very dangerous. But now, both rovers are ready to work.

The mission is called the Mars Exploration Rover mission. *Spirit* and *Opportunity* are looking for proof that there used to be water on Mars. It would have been there almost four billion years ago. Now, NASA is about to find out for sure.

rover: a machine driven by remote control on another planet

Opportunity took many photos of the Martian landscape.

How and Why

Historical events rarely have only one simple cause. Many different things—such as certain events or changing ways of thinking—work together to shape the future. Take a moment to explore some of the things that led to the successful landings of *Spirit* and *Opportunity*.

Chosen Planet

Scientists chose to study Mars because it is the most likely to support life. Most of the planets in our solar system are either too far away or too close to the Sun. This means that most planets are either too hot or too cold. But Mars is the right distance. If there is other life in the solar system, Mars is the most likely place.

Viking I

In 1972, NASA landed *Viking 1* on Mars. The US was the first country to land anything on another planet. *Viking 1* was a lander, which means it was not able to travel around the planet. But it was able to send information and images back to Earth. It lasted more than six years.

Pathfinder and Sojourner

Mars Pathfinder landed 25 years after *Viking 1*. But *Pathfinder* was more than just a lander. *Pathfinder* included a small rover, as well. That rover was named *Sojourner*. *Sojourner* was the first rover to operate on another planet. It drove more than 330 feet (101 meters).

The Search for Water

Life needs water to exist. *Pathfinder*'s goal was to study the dirt on Mars. NASA wanted to know if Mars was once covered in water. *Pathfinder* sent back lots of information. Some of this indicated that there might have been water on Mars. But it wasn't sure. NASA needed another mission. *Spirit* and *Opportunity* were sent to Mars less than 10 years after *Pathfinder*.

What Happened Next

Spirit and *Opportunity* used new technology to land on Mars. It had never been tested in the real world. Nobody knew if it would work. But the new technology succeeded. Neither rover was damaged. The US proved that they could send large rovers to other planets. They could also control the rovers from Earth, and move them across the surface of Mars.

Both *Spirit* and *Opportunity* found important information. Now, NASA knows for sure that Mars once had water. The rovers tested rocks and dirt. These samples told them that Mars used to have a thicker **atmosphere**. Today, Mars's atmosphere is too thin. Nothing can live there. But a long time ago, it might have been as thick as Earth's. If it was, there could have been life.

NASA scientists were very excited by this information. They were also excited about the rovers. *Spirit* and *Opportunity* had proven that the US has the most successful space program in the world. People were more interested in space again. The space program became more popular.

DID YOU KNOW?
Spirit and *Opportunity* are about the size of golf carts.

atmosphere: the layer of gas that surrounds a planet

Rovers have to drive over many different types of ground. They must navigate hills, boulders, and sand as they travel.

Ripple Effects

A single event, no matter how big or small it may seem at the time, can have a big impact on the future. The successful landing of *Spirit* and *Opportunity* had many far-reaching effects.

Opportunity

Opportunity is still working on Mars. It has been there for more than 12 years. It is studying many different things. It is still looking for water. It is also studying the weather and the temperature on Mars. But *Opportunity* is getting old. It has been having some problems. Scientists don't know if it will last much longer.

Curiosity

In 2012, another rover landed on Mars. It is named *Curiosity*. It is the largest rover so far. *Curiosity* is about the size of a Mini Cooper. *Curiosity* is looking for **microbes** on Mars. It is also there to study the planet's past.

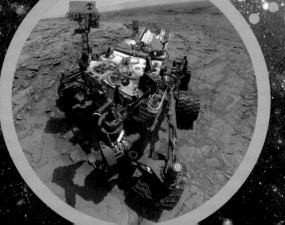

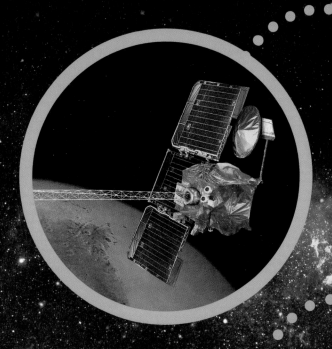

Success

Lots of Mars missions have been successful. Now, NASA wants to send humans to Mars. The information collected from earlier missions will be used to plan a manned mission to Mars.

Mars Missions

Lots of space programs want to send missions to Mars. The European Space Agency and NASA are building missions. Both of these will begin in 2020. These missions will search for life. They will also help to figure out if humans could land on Mars.

microbe: a very small living thing, which can usually only be seen through a microscope

DID YOU KNOW?

Opportunity has driven more than 26 miles (42 kilometers) on Mars.

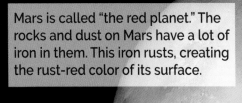

Mars is called "the red planet." The rocks and dust on Mars have a lot of iron in them. This iron rusts, creating the rust-red color of its surface.

PHOBOS AND DEIMOS

Mars has two moons: Phobos and Deimos. They are named after the Greek war god Mars's horses. In Greek, Phobos means "fear" and Deimos means "panic." Asaph Hall, an American astronomer, discovered the two moons in 1877. They don't look very much like our Moon. They are a lot smaller. They are also not completely round. Instead, both of them look more like asteroids. They have lots of craters. Many scientists believe that they were once asteroids. But they got too close to Mars and got trapped in Mars's gravity. Now they orbit Mars.

Humans on Mars?

Spirit and *Opportunity* have taught us a lot about Mars. We know more about its past. We also know more about its soil, weather, and temperature. Only one of the two rovers is still working today. *Spirit* got trapped in soft sand in 2009. It couldn't travel anymore. But it still did experiments on the sand and rocks around it. *Spirit* stopped sending information in 2010.

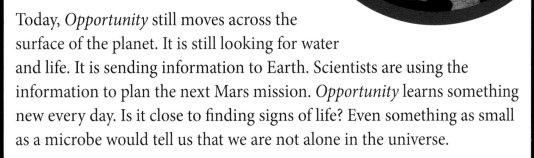

Today, *Opportunity* still moves across the surface of the planet. It is still looking for water and life. It is sending information to Earth. Scientists are using the information to plan the next Mars mission. *Opportunity* learns something new every day. Is it close to finding signs of life? Even something as small as a microbe would tell us that we are not alone in the universe.

NASA learned a lot from *Spirit* and *Opportunity*. One day, that information might help to put a human on Mars.

DID YOU KNOW?

Both rovers were supposed to work for 90 sols, or Martian days. One sol is about 24 hours and 40 minutes. Opportunity has lasted more than 50 times that long.

Quiz

1 What year was *Sputnik* launched?

Answer: 1957

2 Which part on the space shuttle *Challenger* broke when it lifted off?

Answer: An O-ring

3 Who was the first person to walk on the moon?

Answer: Neil Armstrong

4 What country built and launched *Sputnik*?

Answer: The USSR

5 How many moons does Mars have?

Answer: Two, Phobos and Deimos

6 How many astronauts died in the *Challenger* disaster?

Answer: Seven

7 What were *Spirit* and *Opportunity* looking for on Mars?

Answer: Evidence of water

8 What year did the last Apollo mission take place?

Answer: 1972

Glossary

atmosphere: the layer of gas that surrounds a planet

committee: a group of people chosen for a specific reason, or to accomplish a specific task

engineer: someone who designs and builds machines

lunar module: a spacecraft used to transport astronauts to the surface of the Moon

manned: a flight that has a human crew on board

microbe: a very small living thing, which can usually only be seen through a microscope

microelectronics: very small electronic circuits and parts

orbit: the path that something follows as it travels around something else

posthumous: happening after someone's death

rover: a machine driven by remote control on another planet

satellite: a smaller object that orbits a larger object in space

State of the Union: a speech given by the US president to the US Congress, usually delivered once a year

technician: someone who looks after technical equipment

Index

Read More

Crompton, Samuel Willard. *Sputnik/Explorer 1: The Race to Conquer Space.* Milestones in American History. New York, NY: Chelsea House, 2007.

Scott, Elaine. *Space, Stars, and the Beginning of Time: What the Hubble Telescope Saw.* Boston, MA: Clarion Books, 2011.

Edwards, Roberta. *Who Was Neil Armstrong?* New York, NY: Grosset & Dunlap, 2008.

Zoehfeld, Kathleen Weidner. *Apollo 13: How Three Brave Astronauts Survived a Space Disaster.* Totally True Adventures. New York, NY: Random House, 2015.

Baxter, Roberta. *The Challenger Explosion.* History's Greatest Disasters. Minneapolis, MN: ABDO Publishing Company, 2014.

Adamson, Heather. *The Challenger Explosion.* Disasters in History. Mankato, MN: Capstone Press, 2006.

Silverman, Buffy. *Mars Missions: A Space Discovery Guide.* Space Discovery Guides. Minneapolis, MN: Lerner Publishing, 2017.

Rusch, Elizabeth. *The Mighty Mars Rovers: The Incredible Adventures of Spirit and Opportunity.* Boston: Houghton Mifflin Harcourt, 2012.